CATS and KITTENS

Hamlyn
PET CARE
Handbooks

CATS and KITTENS

**Edward Bunting and
Michael Findlay**

HAMLYN

Published by
The Hamlyn Publishing Group Limited
Bridge House, 69 London Road
Twickenham, Middlesex TW1 3SB, England
and distributed for them by
Octopus Distribution Services Limited
Rushden, Northamptonshire NN10 9RZ, England

First published 1987

ISBN 0 600 55136 9

Some of the material in this book
is reproduced from other books published
by The Hamlyn Publishing Group Ltd.

Printed in Hong Kong by Mandarin Offset

Contents

Introduction   8
Choosing and buying   10
Breeds of cat   13
Kittens   23
Training kittens and cats   26
Equipment   29
Feeding   34
General care   38
Outdoor behaviour   44
Indoor behaviour   48
Ailments and health   51
Breeding   56
Showing   59
Useful addresses   61
Index   62

Introduction

The cat has been part of man's household for at least 4,000 years. This might seem a long time, but other animals such as dogs, cattle and sheep were all tamed nearly three times as long ago and this may explain the independent, slightly wild character that is still left in the cat today. Of course, at the same time the cat has a great capacity for affection towards a kind owner.

The story began when the Egyptians tamed African wild cats, at first as mouse and rat catchers. Later, in Roman times, cats were transported to distant parts of the Roman empire and this is how they came to Britain and northern Europe.

Here the cat must have come into contact with another wild species, the European wild cat, which still lives in remoter areas such as the Scottish Highlands. This looks like a larger, fiercer version of an ordinary tabby cat, and it may possibly have interbred with the domestic cat,

The ferocious European wild cat, which is still found in remote areas, is a relation of the domestic cat.

although appearances can deceive and it is very hard to tell exactly if this was so.

Modern man has plenty of enthusiasm for cats, and the cat population is expanding rapidly. At the end of the 1970s, Britain's cat population was estimated at 5 million, or one cat for every five households, figures which had risen to 8 million, nearer one in three households, by 1987.

Pedigree cats are less common: only about one British cat in 16 is a pedigree.

If you decide to have a cat in your home, learn in advance what you must do to keep it in good health and comfort. Raise the kitten kindly and give a thought to safety and accident prevention. You will have a companion whose presence will delight visitors, or members of the family, of all ages.

With modern standards of care, cats usually live for 12 to 16 years or longer. In return for their companionship they require little from you: food, shelter, love and company. They are naturally self-reliant animals and tend to make minimal demands on your time or pocket.

Choosing and buying

There are several places from which you can acquire a new cat or kitten – breeders, pet shops and cat rescue centres are the main sources. One of the best ways to buy a kitten is from a friend whose cat has had a litter, provided you know the household is clean and healthy; this way, you will already be acquainted with the mother cat.

Another way to find kittens is to visit the local vet's surgery: these usually have a notice-board where people can put up advertisements.

In any case it is always best to find out in advance who and where the vet will be who will provide the care your kitten will need. Visit a few if possible, then decide which suits you best.

Terms of purchase

Sometimes you can obtain the kitten on a 'sale or return' basis of one week. This will allow time for a veterinary check, and to see if the new animal is temperamentally suited to its new home. Also, should any signs of serious ill-health be detected, it should be the seller's re-

When choosing a kitten, try to select from a whole litter. Appearance will influence you, of course, but so should behaviour and health. Choose a friendly, frisky kitten rather than a shy one. If any of the kittens is unwell (sneezing, with runny eyes or nose, soiled fur under its tail, flea-bitten, with a poor coat or excessive wax in its ears) it is best to take none of them

sponsibility to rectify the situation, not the new owner's.

If your kitten proves to be infected with an illness or with parasites, do not hesitate or feel embarrassed to return it straight away – the seller needs to know.

Choosing

Any kitten you buy must be six to eight weeks old. If possible see the whole litter, and the mother. Buy only from a litter where all the kittens are free from any signs of illness.

A safe method of choosing is to go for the lively, playful kitten and avoid the shy ones sheltering at the back. But if you know the ways of cats and kittens, you might be able to recognize a shy but well-disposed and healthy specimen who will probably grow into a quiet, friendly pet that will not be too boisterous. Special features to check are:

Eyes should be clear and bright, with no signs of 'weeping'.

Gums pink, not red, with firm, white teeth.

Telling the sex of kittens: a typical female rear end is on the left, a male's on the right

Ears should be clean with no unpleasant smells. With pure white kittens, test for deafness by making sounds from a point outside their field of vision.

Coat clean without matting. Tell-tale signs of fleas are the tiny black dots they leave in the fur. Check for bald patches or flaking skin.

Check also for signs of diarrhoea under the tail. Further veterinary details are given in the Ailments section of this book.

Acquiring an adult cat

Taking on an adult cat can be an advantage if you do not have time to train a kitten, and if you can obtain a well-behaved animal from friends. Other suppliers may be a breeder who has no further use for a particular cat, or an animal welfare organization such as the RSPCA. Some cats simply move in if they find a welcome, and you might never find out where they come from.

If the cat is from an animal shelter or has spent any time astray, you should immediately inspect it for diseases, fleas, mites and so on. Equally important is to take it to a vet for an early and thorough check.

Breeds of cat

Cats vary far less in size and shape than dogs, though they vary more than dogs in colours and patterning. Each of the pedigree breeds of cat has its own special character or personality.

In Britain the organization responsible for recognizing the breeds of cat and for setting the standards to which they are bred is the Governing Council of the Cat Fancy (GCCF). When pedigree kittens are born, the owner registers them with the GCCF and issues a Pedigree Certificate stating the breed of the parents, grandparents and sometimes earlier generations.

Non-pedigree cats

Over many generations, non-pedigree cats have achieved a variety of coat lengths and colours as a result of genetic mixtures. The official name in Britain for the non-pedigree cat is the Domestic Cat.

For identification purposes, non-pedigree cats are best described by coat length (longhair, shorthair and semi-longhair) and by colour – for instance red, tabby, black and blue, together with markings such as white stars on the chest or face, and 'socks' on the legs.

Pedigree cats: longhaired breeds

The Angora is a fine longhaired breed which is known to have existed for many centuries. Long hair appeared as a mutation among the cats of central Turkey centuries ago. By the 16th century travellers took Angoras to France and thence to the rest of Europe. This is a graceful, silky-coated cat, but without the fluffy undercoat of the Persian (see below) and with a slender body. Originally all Angoras were white, but now the range of colours is wide.

The Turkish (called **Turkish Van** in the US) cat is closely related to the Angora. It has a white body with an auburn ringed tail and auburn smudges above the eyes; and it enjoys a swim!

CATS and KITTENS

The Turkish cat is unusual among cats in enjoying swimming

The Maine Coon is an old American breed. It has short legs with a squat body and a square head. Originally a tabby, it now has a wide range of colours.

The Norwegian Forest cat looks very like the Maine Coon but is almost certainly a separate stock. This, too, is a very old breed, originating in Scandinavia.

The Longhairs This is the official name in Britain for a set of varieties with stocky body type and long hair with a thick undercoat. They are often called **Persians**. The legs are comparatively short, the head is rounded with small ears placed well apart, and the nose is short and almost 'pushed in'. Because of their long hair they sometimes seem to look cross, but Persians are in fact good-natured.

The range of colour varieties is vast. Self colours (when the whole cat is just one colour) include white, black, blue, chocolate, lilac, red and cream. Bicoloured cats are a combination of white with one colour, for instance red and white. There are many patterned longhairs, such as Silver Tabby, Brown Tabby and Red Tabby.

Above: *an Orange-eyed White Longhair (Longhair types are widely referred to as Persian);* **below**: *a Shell Cameo cat*

A pair of Chinchilla Longhairs

Particoloured varieties are also available, such as Tortoiseshell (mixed orange and black), Tortoiseshell and White, and Tortoiseshell and Tabby. The Chinchilla is a particularly attractive type of cat, with a white coat, each hair being tipped with black. A stronger degree of black tipping produces the grey effect known as Smoke.

Whites are interesting for their eyes: in some cats both eyes are blue, in others both are orange, and there are also Odd-eyed Whites, a recognized variety. Pure White cats may be deaf.

A Bluepoint Colourpoint Longhair

Colourpoint Longhairs are Persians with the colouring of Siamese cats. In America they count as a separate breed and are called **Himalayans**.

The Birman is similar in appearance to the Colourpoint Longhair, but the breed has characteristic white 'gloves' on all four feet and comes in only four colour varieties – seal, chocolate, blue and lilac. It is known as the Sacred Cat of Burma and according to legend the first Birman was a temple cat in the ancient South-east Asian kingdom of the Khmers. He belonged to a saintly priest whose soul migrated into the cat after his death, whereupon the gods gave the cat white feet as a mark of blessing.

The Balinese is a longhaired Siamese and is available in all the colour patterns found in the Siamese varieties. The hair is not as full as in the Persians, lacking the thick undercoat.

A Seal Point Balinese cat

Pedigree cats: shorthaired breeds

British Shorthairs are compact and powerful with a deep body and full chest. They have short, strong legs and rounded paws, and a short, thick tail. The head is massive and round, with a firm chin and a straight nose. The eyes are round and set well apart, and the fur is short and dense.

These cats are the closest lookalikes to the ordinary non-pedigree cat, but breeders have exaggerated the stockiness or 'cobbiness' of the body. They have also selected for denser fur with a richer colour. Colours are as varied as in Persians.

European Shorthairs are an almost identical series to the British varieties.

This sturdy cat is a pedigree Brown Tabby Shorthair

The Manx cat is born with no, or only a vestigial, tail

American Shorthairs In general, pet cats in America have a slightly more slender, athletic form than the average British cat, and the same is true of the pedigree cats. Again, there is a dazzling range of colours and patterns. There is even a wire-haired variety, with a crimped coat like a terrier's!

Manx As it has no tail, the Manx is bred for roundness of shape with a short back and long hind legs. The head is round and the cat lopes like a rabbit. For showing, a Manx must have no trace of a tail, either to the sight or the touch. This is known as a rumpy Manx. The names 'rumpy-riser', 'stumpy' (or 'stubby') and 'longy' refer to varying lengths of stunted Manx tail.

Some Manx kittens die before birth, and some are born deformed so they have to be put to sleep. Despite this a healthy Manx is known for its intelligence and its ability to jump, climb trees and hunt just as well as if it had a tail to help it balance.

Rex There are two distinct Rex breeds, both deriving from the south-west of England. The **Cornish Rex** has a curly coat with a fairly full, plush texture. It is bred to a slightly oriental body type and is a lithe, athletic cat. The **Devon Rex** has a shorter coat and looks almost hairless. Its head has a decidedly 'pixyish' look.

CATS and KITTENS

A Devon Rex, with its unmistakably large ears and sparse curly coat

Japanese Bobtail This is recognized for showing in America. Its tail is only a few inches long, with bushy hair like a rabbit's tail.

Scottish Fold Shown in America but not Britain, this cat has forward-folded ears. The breed is healthy and robust, being descended from Scottish farm cats, but can have skeletal problems.

Abyssinian This is an ancient breed, often with pointed ear tufts and head stripes, always with large ears and an alert, lynx-like appearance. In most Abyssinians the colour is like that of a wild rabbit, but new shade varieties are developing. Although it looks like a wild animal, it is gentle-natured. **Somali cats** are long-haired Abyssinians.

Russian Blue The colour called blue in cats is really a dilute form of black. A finely-built cat with a wedge-shaped head, the Russian Blue has a soft, very silky coat with a marvellous silver sheen.

Korat This breed has been kept pure and looks exactly as it did 600 years ago in Siam, to judge from illustrations in

This lynx-like appearance is typical of the Abyssinian cat

books preserved from the ancient kingdom. It has a silver-blue coat and a heart-shaped face.

Burmese A rare and highly-prized cat, this was originally either blue or brown, but now there is a variety of colours. In Britain the body is like a Siamese in shape, but in America the breed is more like the American Shorthair.

Siamese These cats almost certainly did originate in Siam (now Thailand). They are instantly recognizable and the most famous of pedigree breeds of cat. The eyes are a clear blue. The body colour is always paler than the 'points' (the feet, tail, ears and face mask). The commonest point colours are seal (brown), blue, chocolate (dark brown), lilac, red, tabby and tortoiseshell.

Most people admire the Siamese cats for their lithe bodies and svelte movements. They are more lively, affectionate and noisy than other types of cat and can be almost dog-like, for they will happily retrieve objects and go for walks on a lead. American breeders like the Siamese's lankiness and toughness so much that they have deliberately exaggerated this character in their cats. But there are those who find the Siamese strange and a little too outlandish for comfort.

CATS and KITTENS

An Oriental Shorthaired Black, an exotic cat with the slinky body shape of a Siamese

Oriental Shorthair Besides the cats we know as Siamese, cat-lovers in ancient Siam used to keep cats of the same body type (which is called oriental) but without the pointed colour pattern. There were cats of pure black, white, brown, blue and shaded silver, and there were bicolours (white plus one colour). All these cats had yellow or green eyes instead of the blue of a point-coloured Siamese.

In the West, these cousins of the Siamese went through a phase of being unfashionable during the early part of the present century, but now they are once more popular.

A Foreign White with her kitten

Kittens

Although your kitten will adapt well to a new home, it will miss its mother at first and you should take care to prepare your home and make a welcome for it. If the kitten is a present for a child, Christmas and birthdays can be noisy times and it is advisable to introduce the young kitten a few days later, when the atmosphere has returned to normal. Aim to collect the new kitten when you are free to give it as much attention as possible.

In the meantime, make the acquaintance of the vet of your choice and fix an appointment for the initial health check. When the kitten is about 12 weeks old it will need another appointment for its first vaccination, plus a second round of general checking.

How to pick up a kitten The mother cat carries her kittens safely by the scruff of the neck, and you can do so for a few seconds, but if you have to carry or hold the kitten for longer, support its tail end with one hand and the chest with the other.

Settling in

When you bring your kitten home, shut all windows and doors and ensure that the house is safe for a young,

A simple bed adapted from a cardboard box will suffice as a kitten's first bed

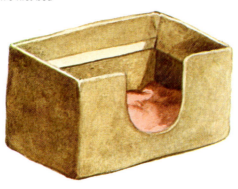

inquisitive animal. Spaces under furniture that could become traps should be blocked off. Cover fireplaces and do not leave clothes hanging to dry before an open fire. Ensure that the kitten will not get into the fire, the refrigerator, the washing machine or other household appliances. Do not leave rubber bands, buttons, needles, pins or other small objects where the kitten could play with them and swallow them.

Building confidence Shut the kitten in one room until it gets used to being there, and make sure that children behave gently and quietly in its presence. Keep under-threes out of the room until it has settled in. All children must be taught to leave a sleeping kitten alone: it needs time to sleep, as well as play.

Once the kitten has overcome its initial fears, it will amuse itself for hours with simple, cheap toys such as ping-pong balls, cores of toilet rolls and woolly stuffed toys.

Other pets These should be shut in a separate room the day the new kitten comes. After an hour they will have grown accustomed to the scent: let them into the kitten's room while holding the kitten in your hand. Make sure you are there to supervise the whole introduction period, which can be brief.

Always support a kitten or cat's weight from underneath when you lift or carry it

Kittens are endlessly resourceful in their play: forethought can save you exasperation!

Exploration A new kitten should be kept in the chosen room – this is usually the kitchen – for about a week. If you decide to allow it outside, you may still find it best to keep it indoors for a few weeks as it gradually explores the new home. It will be inquisitive and will soon learn the way around. Then you can accompany it on its first trip outside – and back. Go with the cat for the first few outings; this will give a sense of security.

Feeding the new kitten

Start by feeding the same diet as the breeder used, if you know it. This will reduce the risk of stomach upsets by over-feeding or supplying too rich a menu. Amounts are shown in the section on Feeding.

If you have to look after a kitten or kittens that have been separated from their mother before the right age (six to eight weeks), you should seek expert advice as to their care. Hand rearing can be successful if correctly done, but skill and patience are needed. Hygiene and sterilization are of the utmost importance. More details of hand rearing are given in the section on Feeding.

Training kittens and cats

The cat's training must start from kittenhood, and has to be based on kindness and a friendly relationship. The cat is an intelligent animal with acute senses, but it is impossible to train it in the same way as dogs, who seem to enjoy displaying obedience almost for its own sake.

Cats learn just as much as dogs, but it is much more in the line of household rules and codes of behaviour than in 'tricks'.

You can reprimand a cat with a stern tone of voice, or slap one hand with a rolled-up newspaper; but never shout at it or slap it. A good deterrent when you catch it in the act of misbehaving is to squirt it with a water pistol – it will simply not realize that you are the cause of the squirting and associate it only with the action. (See also section on Outdoor behaviour.) But you must be prepared to keep a constant watch if you go in for this type of training, and you must not mind looking faintly ridiculous to other humans!

Toilet training

Your kitten will use a litter tray almost instinctively. If it is already eight weeks old when you acquire it, it may have learnt to use a litter tray in its first home. All that is necessary is to place a tray where it can easily find it.

Effective toilet training is another good reason to confine a kitten to one room for its first week. It will not 'lose' the tray; once an accident has occurred in a distant part of the house, the kitten may return there.

It is important to change the litter as often as it is soiled, for cats are very fastidious animals and a tray that is not cleaned may put them off.

For outdoor training, move the tray a short distance each day towards the door, and then outside; after a few days, the cat will begin to use the garden instead.

Empty the litter tray and disinfect it each day. You can

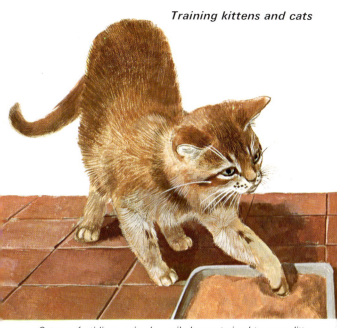

Cats are fastidious animals, easily house-trained to use a litter tray

use a commercial cat litter (those based on Fuller's earth have many advantages) or else peat, soil, wood shavings or sawdust.

Training to come when called

Cats very easily learn to know their names so that almost all cats come when called. The great advance on this is to train a cat so that you can be sure it will come straight away, every time. Reward it with stroking and perhaps a little treat to eat, and you can develop this very useful habit. Repeat the training at intervals throughout the cat's life, and it will respond reliably.

No go areas

The cat will learn to keep off the furniture, or out of the living room, if you establish from the beginning where it will not be allowed to go. Firmly check every time it tries to climb on a chair or enter an area where it is not supposed to go.

Training not to scratch furniture

It may require patience and a sustained effort, but you can teach the cat not to scratch the furniture. You must ensure that it has somewhere where it *can* scratch – a scratching post, or a tree for example; you must be constantly on the watch to catch it in the act; and you must be ready with your reprimand or chosen deterrent.

Training not to scratch people

Surprisingly many adults allow a cat to tread on them with claws outstretched, perhaps rightly recognizing this as a sign of affection. The problem arises when the cat does this to someone who definitely does not like it – children for example. Therefore it is best to show the cat from the start that this type of scratching, too, is not allowed.

Handling and grooming

Make sure that the kitten is handled each day, so it will grow used to the human touch. Kind handling can then lead gently to the introduction of grooming. Longhaired cats need every bit of help you can give them to learn to regard grooming as an extension of affectionate handling. This process must be started in kittenhood.

Its own bed, plus a grooming brush (and comb for a longhair), and claw clippers are essential accessories for your cat

Equipment

Little equipment is needed to care for cats, but the basics are a bed, bowls, a litter tray, grooming equipment and a carrying basket. You will get scores of ideas about things to buy for your cat or kitten in the first five minutes you spend in a pet shop – try going there without any money for a 'practice' visit first!

Bedding

Provide a special bed for a kitten, and train it to sleep there always. A small cardboard box will probably serve best at first. This must be in a warm spot free from draughts, and have a warm, soft lining such as a blanket or pillow. It is advisable to discourage kittens from sleeping on your own bed.

You can make a cat's bed yourself out of wood, or you can buy one made of wicker, fibreglass or fabrics. For a temporary bed, cardboard boxes will do.

The simplest beds are open-topped, with a step in the side for an entrance. You can also buy or build a covered bed like a sleeping compartment, complete with its own roof; these are useful if there is no convenient niche under a table or the stairs to cover in the sleeping cat.

Grooming equipment

For all cats, you need a fairly stiff brush, preferably one with natural bristles. For longhairs you have to have a stout metal comb with wide intervals between the teeth. A fine-toothed 'flea comb' is always useful whether for actually catching fleas or just for giving a refined grooming. You also need a pair of curved scissors to cut through tangled fur. Cotton buds are needed for ear care. A pair of claw clippers complete the cat's essential manicure set.

Collars and harnesses

A special elasticated collar will prevent a climbing cat from getting suspended in a tree, and this can carry an owner's identification disc or tube. You can also fit a bell to warn birds of the cat's approach. Some owners,

A bell on a kitten's collar will let you – and the birds – know where your pet is

especially of Siamese cats, train their animals to go for walks in a harness and lead.

Toys

A huge range of toys is available, facilitating play and exercise. Many of them are stuffed animals containing catnip. This plant, also called catmint, has a thrilling effect on most cats, sometimes an intoxicating one, and this can be dangerous if they live near traffic or are likely to climb on dangerous ledges or go where there are unfriendly animals or people.

Scratching posts

These again are either bought or made. Their value is limited unless you are prepared to make a determined effort to train the cat to scratch on the post and nowhere else in the home. Training must be from the very start. Every cat has a biological need to scratch; it gets rid of the flaking ends of unworn claws, but the behaviour is also part of its method of marking territory.

One way to protect a piece of furniture that the cat has taken to scratching is to fix a sheet of plastic over the area at risk. Cats do not like the feel of plastic sheeting and will leave the furniture alone.

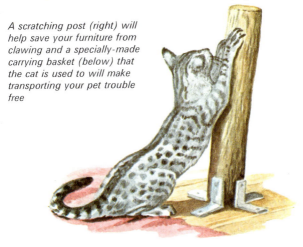

A scratching post (right) will help save your furniture from clawing and a specially-made carrying basket (below) that the cat is used to will make transporting your pet trouble free

Carrying basket

Probably the best investment, though overlooked by countless first-time kitten owners, is a well-made carrying basket of wicker or fibreglass. At short notice you can make do with cardboard boxes punched or cut to provide breathing holes, and in an emergency a zip-up holdall will do: but the right way is to have the basket ready from the start.

Let the kitten play in it from its earliest days, and it will not be afraid to go in it when the time comes to use it. In fact this happens fairly often: visits to friends, journeys to

the boarding cattery or to shows, and trips to the vet –
planned and unplanned.

Feeding bowls

Many owners find cats prefer their water to be some
distance away from their food bowl. Place the feeding
bowl on a mat or on newspaper, to facilitate cleaning as
cats often lift the food to eat it outside the bowl.

Automatic cat feeders are available, which store meals
and 'feed' the cat for you by opening a tight-fitting lid at
the time or times you set. These enable you to go out for a
longer time.

Litter tray

Use a litter tray that is deep enough to hold several inches
of litter, and has enough space for the cat. Covered litter
trays help to prevent spillage of litter and may be more
appealing to some cats.

Cat flap

Many cat owners fit a cat flap to their outside door – or
window. This will allow the cat to go in and out whenever

*Timed cat-feeding systems mean you can be absent for up to
two mealtimes*

Cat flaps mean your cat does not have to be cooped up, or your house insecure, while you are out

it likes, without you having to open the door or window; but beware: it also lets other cats in if you aren't watching! And it must be located sufficiently far from the door or window handle to prevent burglars from reaching in and letting themselves in. Obviously, the flap must also be low enough for the cat to reach.

To train the cat to use the cat flap, it is usually enough to prop it open initially and gradually reduce the size of the prop. There is a type of cat flap that swings only outwards, and will not let the cat in again unless you train it to open the flap by lifting it with a paw. Another type of cat door is not a flap but a ring of plastic triangles fixed round the rim of the hole; they are flexible and their points meet at the centre. The cat simply pushes through, parting the plastic triangles.

Electro-magnetic and electronically operated cat flaps are available and these are not massively expensive; they will open only to the cat that carries a special device, usually attached to its collar. To all other comers, they remain shut.

Feeding

Cats are basically meat eaters (carnivores) but they often eat a little grass if free to roam, or if you grow grass for them indoors. It helps their digestion, though it is not thought to be of nutritional importance to the cat.

Generally, adult cats are fed twice daily; the daily food ration should be about 150–250 g (5–8 oz). This may be increased in the case of pregnant females or those suckling kittens.

Types of cat food

Good quality proprietary foods make by far the simplest diet from the owner's point of view. These and the laws relating to them have been developing for many generations, and the products have come to be very reliable, provided you follow the manufacturer's instructions on the container about how much and how often to feed. They contain all the required nutrients such as vitamins and minerals which might be lacking in a diet of fresh meat or scrap foods.

Canned foods are well balanced and there is a good range of varied flavours. These are moist, so the cat will be generally less thirsty.

Semi-moist foods are less expensive because they incorporate some vegetable protein instead of meat. They keep well in the bowl without drying out or losing texture, and they taste good to cats. You may need to balance the diet by giving canned or fresh foods from time to time.

Dry foods are cheaper too. The cat will need at least a large cupful of fluid to drink each day – water, milk or gravy.

Fresh foods Variety of food is important to cats, and it is good to give fresh foods occasionally. If you keep a large number of cats, a full diet of fresh foods, once you have worked one out, will save you money. Raw minced beef, sold for human consumption, is safe and free from

Food and drink for your pet should be kept in a familiar place

internal parasites, and cats find it delicious. Serve liver, heart and kidneys cooked or raw, but fish must be cooked – boiled or steamed. Cooked rabbit and chicken, and raw or scrambled eggs, make a satisfying change.

Occasionally a cat will become 'addicted' to certain foods, particularly raw liver, which can be harmful if fed over long periods. Firmly steer the diet back towards greater variety.

It is dangerous to feed cats on dog food. Canned dog foods, if fed for a prolonged period, can cause serious illness to a cat.

Drinking

Water should be left down at all times. The amount the cat will drink varies with the type of food it is eating at the time.

Milk is wrongly thought to be an essential for cats: it is not a natural component of the adult cat diet, and actually causes physical upsets to many cats, particularly orientals. For these, it is best avoided.

Feeding kittens

In general, very young kittens are best left to their mother's care, and it is dangerous to interfere in any way until the kittens are weaned. Kittens cease to drink their mother's milk by the age of eight weeks, although they may begin to wean gradually from four or five weeks.

From weaning to 12 weeks, kittens should have a minimum of four small meals daily – each approximately 25 g (1 oz). From 12–16 weeks, three meals daily will suffice, and kittens over 16 weeks can have two meals daily. See also section on kittens.

A tiny kitten left motherless, for whatever reason, before it would normally be weaned (at about six weeks) will have to be fed a milk substitute by dropper or proprietary kitten-feeding equipment. Stroke it gently with damp cotton wool as a substitute for its mother's licking

Hand rearing

If a kitten is abandoned or orphaned, you might have to take over its care from the mother, and in the first five weeks of life this is called hand rearing. It is a difficult task and if possible you should avoid the need for it by fostering the kittens to a mother who is producing milk but has only a few kittens (or none) of her own.

In hand rearing it is crucial to observe the strictest rules of hygiene and sterilize your equipment very carefully. The mother's milk gives a kitten valuable antibodies that protect it from infection. Without its mother's milk, a kitten lacks antibodies and may easily die if it catches an infection. Seek advice about hand rearing from a vet or an experienced breeder.

The equipment for hand rearing is simple. You can use an eye dropper to place drops of milk formula in the kitten's mouth. Otherwise you can buy a medical syringe and adapt this, by replacing the needle with a short length of fine tubing; or you can buy a specially manufactured kitten feeding bottle at the pet shop. The amount starts at about a teaspoonful per feed, in the first week, fed every two hours. Gradually increase the amount per feed, and work down to a frequency of four feeds per day.

Milk formula for hand rearing Use either of these preparations:
1 Human baby milk food at double normal strength.
2 A mixture of the following: 1 teacup of fresh cow's milk, $\frac{1}{4}$ teacup of single cream, $\frac{1}{4}$ egg yolk, 1 drop of cod liver oil, $\frac{1}{4}$ teaspoon of sterilized bone meal. Stir to a uniform consistency and serve at body temperature. It may be stored in a refrigerator.

Hand weaning

Once the hand reared kitten has survived its first four or five weeks and is doing well, you have to wean it off its first milk formula, and gradually introduce adult food.

Milk formula for weaning After four or five weeks of age, the kittens can be fed on any of the following:
1 Either of the above.
2 Proprietary powder from a pet shop.
3 Milk mixed with raw egg yolk.
4 Puppy biscuit simmered in milk.

Serving the cat's meal

1 Feed your pet at the same time and place every day.
2 Place a newspaper or mat under the food dish. Many cats drag their food from the dish and eat it on the floor.
3 Let your pet eat undisturbed.
4 Leave food out for at least an hour; most cats eat their meals slowly.
5 Avoid sudden changes to your cat's diet.
6 Never give spiced food.
7 Most cats like bones to eat and play with, but do not give fish bones or chicken bones. Also avoid any sharp bones.

General care

Compared to other animals, the domestic cat needs little in the way of attention providing the owner supplies the few basic requirements.

Comfort

All cats should have their own beds; this gives them a place to rest quietly and get away from humans for a while. The bed should be draught-free itself, and it should be placed in a quiet, unobtrusive spot such as under a table or below the stairs.

Hygiene

Cats should have their own feeding and water bowls and these should be washed separately from family crockery. Include a spoon and tin opener with the cat's special equipment, washed separately from your own utensils.

Remember that certain household disinfectants and antiseptics are toxic to cats. Dettol, TCP and some other brands contain chlorinated phenols, which can make a cat badly ill. Their manufacturers will not thank you for allowing a cat to be poisoned through inappropriate use of their products. Domestos is one brand that is safe for cats, and there are others.

Grooming

Every cat should be brushed daily. This is essential for Longhairs, which should also be combed daily to remove knots and mats of fur. The great art is to get the cat to like it (see section on Training kittens and cats).

All cats will continue to groom themselves (or each other) even though you do brush and comb them, so it is not normally necessary to bath them. The exceptions are (a) when showing, and (b) when the vet directs a medicated bath.

Exercise

As a species, cats are rather lazy, for in the wild they have always been wait-and-see predators. You can encourage them to take exercise: cats will readily play with toys (see

Cats groom themselves and each other (above) but still need a thorough daily brushing by their owner (right). **Below**: Once fully grown and less destructive, a cat's cardboard box bed can be replaced by one of the many specially designed types that are on sale

section on Equipment), and you may wish to build a run (see section on Indoor behaviour).

Neutering

Every vet will recommend that you have your pet kitten neutered. Many of the reasons will be clear from the Behaviour and Breeding sections of this book, but in short, cats tend to fight strange cats, partly from sexual motivation and partly in territorial disputes, and this can be minimized by neutering toms at the age of about five months. Stud cats (males kept for breeding) should be kept confined at all times in special accommodation. Female cats should also be neutered at the same age, if not destined for breeding; this will minimize straying, and of course unwanted kittens.

Vaccinations

Have your kitten vaccinated and do not forget the yearly booster – this also gives a chance for your vet to examine the cat and for you to ask any questions which may occur to you.

Secure cat travelling baskets in a variety of sizes, materials and prices are widely available and a sound buy

Though not ideal, cats can be carried in a zip-up bag – with their heads outside, of course!

Holidays and travel

Bear in mind holiday time; it is not always possible or desirable for a neighbour to drop in to feed a cat left at home, and it is much preferable to have it cared for by a good boarding cattery. Remember that cats cannot be taken abroad on holiday (as an anti-rabies precaution) and that few hotels are geared to feline guests. Inspect the cattery before booking, and do this well in advance as these places get booked up very quickly, especially in high season.

Most cats make good, if noisy and nervous, travellers. For safety they should be confined in a proper cat carrier; in emergencies a zip-up bag will suffice. Some cats will travel happily on a harness and lead but only if accustomed to it. Sedation can be given, but should be avoided if at all possible.

New homes

Cats moving to new homes cause many owners concern. Remember, however, that cats attach themselves to humans, not property. For the first week or so, keep the cat confined to the house; this is an occasion where mild sedation may be helpful. Then allow it, if this is your wish, to go outside, preferably supervised at first and for short periods, gradually becoming longer. The cat will not bolt, but rather gradually enlarge its radius of exploration so that it can find its way home. An identity tube or disc on a collar will help your peace of mind.

Other animals

Cats, and especially kittens, will integrate well with other animals such as non-aggressive dogs and other cats. Generally it is best not to try a gradual introduction. Although it sounds hazardous, it is better to make an abrupt introduction, making a fuss of the residents rather than the newcomer; they will quickly establish their own order of seniority. (See also the section on Kittens.)

Examining your cat

A thorough weekly examination of your cat will pay dividends. Lift the lips and check teeth and gums; make sure there are no excessive tartar deposits on the outside of the cheek teeth and that the gums are a normal pink and not inflamed.

Check the eyelids, especially if there is evidence of tears; if the lid-linings are red, bathe with a human eye-wash and seek help in 48 hours unless they become clear. Clean off any extra wax in the ears with a cotton bud moistened in olive oil. If this is copious or smelly, seek veterinary help.

Examine the claws carefully, especially on the front feet in the older cat; inability to strop these may result in overgrowth which you can cut a little using toenail clippers or specially made claw clippers. Examine the skin for bare patches or sores; early treatment of skin disease is very worthwhile.

Fleas

There is positively no shame or dishonour in having a cat with fleas – central heating and wall-to-wall fitted carpets

Cats can be let into the garden without fear of them running away after being kept indoors in a new home for a week or so

are a boon to these insects. Sprays and powders, and specially impregnated collars, are available at every pet shop.

Outdoor behaviour

Cat behaviour is one of the great fascinations of cat lovers. Domestic cats mimic exactly the behaviour of their large wild counterparts. The cat is designed for hunting, and is particularly well suited to dim-light activity; hence it is generally regarded as a nocturnal animal.

Cats have very highly developed hearing, enabling

If your cat encounters small animals you must not be surprised or upset of its hunting nature emerges, however well fed it is

them to detect prey well before seeing it, and their refined senses of smell and taste account for their reluctance to eat unfresh food. They also probably protect cats from swallowing poisonous material.

Hunting behaviour

Cats have the ability to stalk prey for long periods unseen and unheard, and their claws and teeth, together with their extra supple, muscular bodies, explain their success as animals of prey.

Hunting technique, however, is learnt behaviour. Cats do not fully know how to do it by instinct alone. With domestication, some mother cats have lost some of their enthusiasm for hunting and no longer teach it to their young. So if your kitten's mother is not a hunter, the kitten may not be one either.

If you are a bird lover as well as a cat lover, you can train a young cat not to catch birds. Make a 'lure' with the feathers of a bird it has killed, and tie this to the end of a long thread or string. Hide yourself in a suitable place and let the cat find the lure in the garden. Whenever it attacks the lure, direct a well-aimed shot at it with a water pistol. Regular sessions of this type of training will put the cat off bird-stalking without it associating the punishment with you.

Tree climbing

Most members of the cat family use trees as vantage points for eating and resting, and as hiding places from which to leap down and attack unsuspecting animals below. This is how the domestic cat came by its ability to climb, and to land upright after a fall.

Owners sometimes underestimate the cat's skill in tree climbing, and raise the alarm when they see it apparently stuck in a tree. Experience has shown that in nine cases out of ten the cat will work out a way to get out of the tree within 24 hours. You can encourage it down by placing food at the base of the tree, which should bring it home without the fire brigade!

The folklore about cats having nine lives may derive from their well developed sense of balance and their remarkable ability to get out of tricky situations of this kind.

Territories and calling

Domestic cats are strongly territorial. An unneutered ('entire') tom reaches sexual maturity at an age of six to eight months and then he begins to establish his own territory. He marks out his own land with drops of urine (this is called 'spraying') and will battle fiercely with other cats to defend or increase his domain.

Town toms will go for the biggest area they can lay claim to and defend, which may extend across several gardens. In country districts, an entire tom may take a square mile or so!

Females, too, hold territories, though these are smaller. An entire female will start to 'call' early in the first spring after she has attained the age of five months. At this time she ceases to defend her territory against toms and actively seeks their company. She attracts them from far away with a special scent, and by uttering a long, monotonous call. Sometimes, especially in Siamese or part Siamese or any oriental cats, it is more of a howl. Visiting toms will hang around her territory and you will have to put up with their spraying. There may be fights in the area of your home, and much caterwauling at night.

Cats mark their territory by spraying, rubbing scent glands against objects and scratching

Unneutered toms can be very fierce and noisy

Behaviour of neutered cats

If neutered in kittenhood, the behaviour of cats is almost the same whether male or female, at least from the practical point of view of running the household. Their territories are much smaller, toms do not spray and females do not call. Territorial fights, though they may still happen, are much less of a problem.

Toms tend to grow larger than females (just as in the unneutered condition), and a female is generally more dainty, but both are affectionate and amenable when neutered. They tend to spend more of their time at home.

There is some truth in the observation that neutered cats, of both sexes, become inactive and lazy when they grow older. Some grow overweight or even obese. Obviously, it is partly a matter of discipline in feeding, but there are other ways in which you can help. If you spend some time with your cat each day, play with it and exercise it, this will be enough to stimulate its interest in its surroundings, and so a neutered cat is not necessarily a lazy one.

Indoor behaviour

The housebound cat

Today there are many situations where a cat spends its whole life housebound, and if the right arrangements are made this is not cruel and can work perfectly. Some people disapprove and many are surprised to see a natural prowling animal living indoors, but it is a definite feature of urban life and it is here to stay. It is best to try and understand how a cat experiences indoor life, and to help it adapt to this situation. Try to think of ways to prevent boredom, for bored cats can become destructive, for example by excessive scratching of furniture.

Reasons for containment

Safety is the main argument in favour of keeping the cat in. In cities, free-roaming cats are constantly exposed to a formidable array of dangers. Traffic accidents involving cats happen all too often, and there are cat thieves about in any city. Besides this there are large cat populations and so a prowling cat is very likely to meet others and pick up infections.

Prowling cats also eat mice or rats, or food from dustbins and tips, especially in the urban environment. All these foods are frequently infected with parasites and other illnesses. Territorial fights and unwanted pregnancies are extra complications that every cat lover wishes to avoid.

In the US, these reasons are taken far more seriously by the general public than in Britain, and a large proportion of American cats are kept indoors.

Finally, pedigree cats have to be kept under strict control for reasons of purity of breeding, and because the cats are usually valuable and must be protected from thieves.

Housebound cats that are not being kept for breeding purposes must be neutered during kittenhood. Confining an uncastrated tom or queen leads to serious behavioural problems. With breeding cats, this problem is solved because the owner plans and organizes a programme of selective mating and breeding.

Obviously, extra attention to hygiene is needed, and litter trays should be cleaned and disinfected scrupulously. For kittens, feeding is a problem as they will not be able to last out the day if their owners are out at work. Fresh food, if left out, may go bad or become unpalatable to the kittens. The solution lies in semi-moist foods, which keep well in the bowl, and in dry foods. Automatic feeders may also be useful (see Feeding section).

Indoor plants The indoor cat's diet should be enhanced by growing grass in trays or pots. You could try growing some catnip too. Cats need to eat some green vegetation

A well thought out and equipped run helps exercise and entertain a confined cat

and without a tray of grass they may eat your houseplants. Apart from being a nuisance to you, this is dangerous for the cat, for some houseplants are poisonous to them. Dieffenbachias and poinsettias are the commonest causes of houseplant poisoning, but there are several other species that poison cats. Some cacti cause serious problems because their tiny spines harm the cat's digestive system.

Exercise
Your cat will naturally try all the windows, so ensure that these are catproof, and that any balconies are safe. To save your furniture, you could provide an 'adventure playground' of cardboard tubes and boxes, imaginatively carved and assembled. Toys are vitally important in an indoor cat's life.

Cat breeders construct outdoor pens for their studs to live in, and this is a good idea for the ordinary pet owner if you have a little outdoor space available. Build it with timber and wire mesh, with shelves for jumping, and use trees – living ones or cut branches – to make the pen more attractive.

For the times that you do spend with your cat, try training it to walk on a lead. Often this works better with a harness.

An excellent way to prevent a cat from becoming bored at home without human company all day is to provide a companion pet. In this situation, two cats are often better than one.

Cats and children
Children of three years and under cannot be expected to know the correct way to handle a cat, so close supervision is the best way to guarantee safety. However, kittens who grow where toddlers are about become astonishingly tolerant of human infants!

There is a common belief that cats like to sleep in a baby's cot or pram, and may smother the baby. This has, however, never been proved. Obviously, nets are available as a precaution, and cats can be shut out of rooms where babies sleep.

Ailments and health

Vaccinations will protect cats well against the killer disease of panleucopaenia (feline infectious enteritis) and against the two forms of cat 'flu (feline viral rhinotracheitis and calicivirus). The vaccinations are double and are given from about ten weeks of age; they are free from side effects. Once a kitten is vaccinated, yearly boosters are required to continue full protection. These diseases are more likely where many cats are confined together – such as boarding establishments or shows – but can equally affect a cat at home since they can be airborne or carried by foot.

Feline leukaemia This is a virus disease which is a serious scourge. At this moment there is no protection and pedigree kittens should be bought from certified leukaemia-free parents. The symptoms are very varied; all affected cats are obviously unwell and a veterinary surgeon should be consulted, but there is no treatment.

Urinary disease This is common in cats; any signs of a great increase in thirst or difficulty in passing urine should suggest urgent veterinary treatment.

Vomiting This symptom is common in cats – often after eating grass. Frequently a felt sausage ('fur-ball') is regurgitated, which is the normal way for cats to expel swallowed fur. Persistent sickness merits attention.

Abscesses These often result from cat fights and puncture wounds; they may need lancing and a dose of antibiotics.

Skin problems These are common, too. The most frequent type is an allergic skin condition often caused by flea bites. A vet will clear the condition, but keep a close

A cat swallows some fur in its constant self-grooming, and occasionally regurgitates fur balls. This is quite normal behaviour and no cause for concern

watch to prevent further flea infestations. Ringworm can also occur, and because of its possible transmission to humans it must be treated quickly.

Eye conditions These are rare, except in injuries from cat fights. If two days bathing in weak salt water does not improve the eye, seek help. 'Haws-up' is not serious but needs veterinary help. The 'haw' is the cat's third eyelid. If visible this may indicate an ailment.

Ear conditions These are indicated by excessive build-up of wax, pain on touching, or any unpleasant smell. Do not be tempted to treat such conditions yourself.

Worms All kittens should be dosed against roundworms – this is often done at vaccination time. Tapeworms are regular parasites in cats that eat rabbits, mice, etc. and those infested with fleas. Although not serious it is wise to worm such cats at least every six months.

Above: *a cat's eye in normal health;* **Centre:** *the third eyelid partly covering the eye is a sign of poor condition;* **below:** *ear scratching is normal feline behaviour, but if done excessively may indicate a problem*

Diarrhoea This is not infrequent in cats and often goes undetected because of their toilet habits. The vast majority of diarrhoea cases are caused by some unsuited dietary component – often milk – and eliminating this often solves the problem. If persistent, veterinary help is needed to treat what may be a digestive infection.

General symptoms of illness

The sick cat usually identifies itself easily. It is unduly lethargic, and may be hot to touch if fevered. It may show signs of pain, especially if handled, and its breathing may be fast or laboured when it is at rest. Even healthy cats may voluntarily deprive themselves of food for up to 48 hours, but avoidance of food for longer periods is a sign that you need the vet.

Cats that hide One awkward problem with sick cats is that in some conditions the cat will respond by trying to hide itself away, for example in a shed or in some bushes. This may occur with injured cats. This behaviour is

An unusually lethargic or warm cat, or one off its food, is probably unwell. If unusual behaviour persists or worsens, see a vet

Unwell cats often become elusive and anti-social, hiding themselves away

thought to originate from life in the wild, when cats had to hide from attackers when too weak to defend themselves. But it can cause a lot of anxiety for the owner, and delay treatment.

Hardship cases

If you have a sick cat and can definitely show proof of financial hardship, you may be able to get free or cheap treatment through the People's Dispensary for Sick Animals (PDSA) or the RSPCA (see addresses at the back of this book).

Breeding

Far too many unwanted kittens are produced each year and then abandoned or destroyed. Don't therefore breed unless you have acquired a pedigree cat for this purpose or unless you have good homes for all kittens beforehand.

It is far better to have your cat neutered by your vet from about five months to prevent unwanted pregnancies.

Pedigree female cats are taken by prior arrangement to a suitable tom (stud) cat when they are in season (or calling). The matings are carefully supervised and the female (queen) stays for about three days.

Cats are pregnant for about nine weeks. During pregnancy, cats should be handled with care, and should have an increase in food allowance, together with any

Kittens are born with their eyes sealed: they open when they are a few days old

New kittens suckle for four to eight weeks

supplements prescribed by your vet. Queens are usually checked three to four weeks after mating and one week before kittening. Cats normally kitten without assistance, but it is wise to inspect her nesting place occasionally in case you need to intervene should the mother appear to be in difficulty. Queens will normally take full care of their litter.

Cats have a well-developed maternal instinct, feeding, grooming and protecting their litters for a number of weeks after birth

At seven weeks old a kitten is almost independent of its mother's nuture and care

Care of the kittens

Handle the kittens gently every day to accustom them to human contact. Kittens are taught to lap (known as weaning) at four to five weeks and start solid food soon after in preparation for their new homes. They are mature at about six months of age but it is unwise to breed them until they are about a year old. Your vet can stop them coming into season (which can occur every three to four weeks) with tablets or an injection.

Deceptively relaxed looking adults in fact keeping a watchful eye on an inquisitive kitten

Showing

Principally cat shows are run under the strict rules of the GCCF (Governing Council of the Cat Fancy) and are for pedigree cats, though quite a few shows have sections nowadays for pet (or non-pedigree) cats. All pedigree cats in such shows must be already registered with the GCCF. Application to show must be made in advance.

Since 1982 the Cat Association of Britain has been running more informal cat shows, while of course still adhering to strict standards of breeding and hygiene. It also caters more readily for the non-pedigree cat owner.

Procedure at the show

On the day of the show all cats are checked by veterinary surgeons to reduce the risk of disease being transmitted at the show; then each cat is penned, separately as a rule.

Each judge and his or her steward visit the cats in sections (classes) and each exhibit is removed from its pen and judged individually, being marked on its quality. Thus the top four or five cats in each class are selected. In some shows the best in each group is chosen as a finale, i.e. best Siamese, best Longhair, best Shorthair.

Most shows clear the hall of spectators until lunch-time to allow the judges to work unhampered. Each exhibit must wear a tally round its neck bearing only a number for identification and the only pen contents allowed are a white blanket, a litter tray and water container, until judging is complete. Cats cannot be removed until the end of the show (usually at about 5 p.m.) unless they fall ill. In that case a veterinary certificate is given to allow the cat to be taken away.

Reasons for exhibiting

Showing is to many a great hobby; it is also important to breeders whose aim is to achieve 'Champion' status for their stock as an indication of excellence. The offspring of champions tend to be considerably more expensive to buy, and stud fees for the use of a Champion stud are also higher. Showing the pet cat is essentially a hobby, for

Rosettes and cups are only the most obvious rewards of successful cat showing

most domestic cats are non-breeding neuters.

In either case showing a cat means an early start, and a long tiring day, and the most critical factor is whether the cat is suited to this life. Never show a pet cat that is upset by travel or showing.

Useful addresses

Cats' Protection League, 17 King's Road, Horsham, West Sussex RH13 5PP.

Feline Advisory Bureau, 350 Upper Richmond Road, London SW15 6TL.

People's Dispensary for Sick Animals, PDSA House, South Street, Dorking, Surrey RH4 2LB.

Royal Society for the Prevention of Cruelty to Animals (RSPCA), The Causeway, Horsham, West Sussex RH12 1HQ.

Cat Association of Britain, CAB Central Office, Hunting Grove, Lowfield Heath, Crawley, West Sussex RH11 0PY.

Governing Council of the Cat Fancy, 4–6 Penel Orlieu, Bridgwater, Somerset TA6 3PG.

Index

Figures in italics refer to illustrations

Abyssinian 20, *21*
American Shorthair 19, 21
Angora 13

Balinese 17, *17*
bedding *28*, 29, 38, *39*
Birman 17
breeding 56–8
British Shorthair 18
Burmese 21

carrying baskets 31–2
Cat Association of Britain 59
cat feeders 32, *32*
cat flaps 32–3, *33*
children and 50
choosing and buying 10–12
collars and harnesses 29–30
Colourpoint Longhair *16*, 17
comfort 38
Cornish Rex 19

Devon Rex 19, *20*
Domestic Cat 13

equipment 29–33
European Shorthair 18
examining 42
exercise 38, 40, 50
exhibiting 59–60

feeding 25, 34–7
feeding bowls 32
fleas 42–3
Foreign White *22*

general care 38–43
Governing Council of the
    Cat Fancy 59
grooming 28, *28*, 29, 38, *39*

hand rearing 25, 36–7
hand weaning 37
handling 28
health 51–5
Himalayan 17
hygiene 38

indoor behaviour 48–50

Japanese Bobtail 20

kittens 23–5, 35, 42, 56, *56*,
    57, 58, *58*
Korat 20–21

litter trays 26, 32
longhaired 13–17, 28
Longhairs 14, *15*, 16–17

Maine Coon 14
Manx 19, *19*

neutering 40, 47
new homes 42, *43*
non-pedigree 13
Norwegian Forest 14

Oriental Shorthair 22, *22*
other animals 42
outdoor behaviour 44–7

Persian
    see Longhairs

Rex 19
Russian Blue 20

Scottish Fold 20
scratching posts 28, 30, *31*
Shell Cameo *15*
shorthaired 18–22
Siamese 17, 21, 22, 30
Somali 20